THE GOD OF
Indeterminacy

POEMS BY
Sandra McPherson

UNIVERSITY OF ILLINOIS PRESS
Urbana and Chicago

D0057316

Publication of this work was supported in part by grants from
the National Endowment for the Arts and the Illinois Arts Council,
a state agency.

This book is printed on acid-free paper.

Library of Congress Cataloging-in-Publication Data
McPherson, Sandra.
    The god of indeterminacy : poems / by Sandra McPherson.
        p.   cm.
    ISBN 0-252-06271-X
    I. Title.
    PS3563.A326G6   1993
    811'.54—dc20   92-14714
                                                         CIP

To Hip Linkchain (Willie Lee Richard, 1936–89),
to John Emmet Todd (1913–90),
and always for Walter Pavlich, "The Spirit of Blue Ink"

The God of Indeterminacy is about aesthetics, even metaphysics, as manifested in some often unlooked-at *corners* of culture in America and more distant places. Or *centers:* a working title for this collection was at one time *The Center in the Corner.* My investigations also led me to curate a quilt show. The reader might find that the center is indeed in the corner or elsewhere, the indeterminate godly place without a name.

S.M.

Contents

THE GOD OF INDETERMINACY

Twelve-Bar Quilt

For the night's last song
binding off the benefit
for the dying bluesman,

his friend Jimmy Johnson
performs in a shirt
made out of blue poly

just like the knit fabric
in the last wide stripe
that chords across the border

of this invention—has on
one of those tight,
everlasting, basement shirts

of flattened color
and glassy fiber
he wears on album covers.

Here it is as bedcover—
albeit sleepless,
the kind of design

or blues that keep you
up at night.
Here it is as bars

that shake the sleeper.
The singer's eyes too
are up, thrown back,

pushed up and back
by bent flats of his guitar.
And his voice goes high,

rises in downtown rafters,
till we feel clothespinned
and people want to know

where to get it,
get it always, what to strip
away, fine tailoring,

the bought bedspread,
how to come by it,
how to be born,

who to be born.
The quilter sews twelve
wide rivers to immerse in:

just beyond gospel,
this violent patch-thing
is the crib quilt for me.

Quilt of Rights

Yes, I do see many of us afraid of scraps,
afraid of their big design.
But once, every quilter knew she had a right
to color and shape, even if she believed in
no known meaning of *pretty.*

It is that maker whom I ask to teach me.

In the Muskogee Flea Market this soul's claim
to color passes to anyone.
She built cloth skylights
and for awhile trusted herself
to fit just blue ones,
clear around a weather of small forms—
birds' eyes, pollen.
But then she guessed her right to sun in windows;
she colored her way to coral panes;
and finally directed all her vistas
to be plaid: plaid elms, plaid storm,
all shoppers and all dogs
tartan and clashing
as was her right.

No shadings between the frenzied and the cool.

But listen, I tell my rocky soul:
the normality of this—.
For it is not done with moods.
It is given with a right to color.

Quilt Top Discovered at the Muskogee Flea Market and Found to Contain Blocks Resembling Certain Designs of Descendants of Maroons in Suriname

Brief, direct stitches, wild eye.
Her knots still eddy
from finger-winding, pulling.

Unblending plaid compilations, like gourd heaps
or melon stripes rolled into a mound,
poppy and tansy-yellow squashes, striated cucumbers, leanings
of December cornstalks still offering
late, secret usefulness.

She measured nothing. But she used
all notions of rough equality
to scissor the unlike prints similar,
then sewed them back together to clash.

In Suriname the Saramaka gossips named
their cloth: *blackbird fat* (for orange lines),
okra water (dark and steaming), *co-wife*
peppered co-wife (pink in honor
of the one who crushed hot chilis
into her co-wife's douche).

And the lowdown condenses,
candid, in these Oklahoma squares:
a handkerchief-sized closetful
of fifty brights, none so small
it can't tell how her comfort
liked to move in it.

So she is glad she told herself this way.

And this: a handwriting
of close, irreproachable stitches
tells her, from the back.

For St. James, Who Said He Was
on Tour with The Emotions

with help from Percy Mayfield

He has just written his first song
and there is a question as to who it is for—
his girl, his Lord, or the lead singer,
his measure, who told him, "Write a song
for yourself." Or for the people.

    "You sing a song that you ask yourself a question
    then you got to answer it."

The silver handspan of the sunset is unusual.
It reminds him of the shine of fields and goats at home.
He doesn't have to wait in the shadow of buildings, of anything.
He wrote his personal lyric this morning.
He is in awe of singing it.

    "Some didn't make it big, that have a breath full of meaning.
    I write to me. I cater the universal."

What are the layers of the night,
stepping into one spotless and single one?—
no airplane lands on sight,
no sparrow shades itself beneath the solar panels,
no wasp catnaps against the eaves
the way a swimmer clings by elbows to the inside of a pool.
And no notes cheat on their words
in the deep regard of night.

"I could sell more sadness than I can joy.
There's more sadness in the world than there is joy."

Can you sing a stanza for Georgia,
voiceless, aphonic, finger-spelling, hushed,
for Georgia, half-breathing, double-gasping,
for Georgia whose voice the doctors took?
(Her visitors/friends/daughters say she blows kisses.)

"I wore sadness instead of just singin' about sadness.
I would wear it, see."

A songmaker's voice knows how to slip.
For all the things he sings have happened,
have slipped around him.
He escapes on his own vowels, no one else's.

"Some imagine beauty and some imagine pain."
"I'm a poet, and my gift is love."

The dead singer's voice shreds at both ends.
Exhaust, hair brushed till it splits.
"In the early days, I would growl.
Now I breaks my words off—people call it a style.
But I was running out of breath, I would write songs that
I wouldn't even sing."

"I promised God I wouldn't write and sing a lie."

He has just written his first song and it is night.
But he has just written his first song

on the road, in flat country reminding him
of plow-opened fields under the city
at home. He carries it into the night
that reminds him of every night
everywhere.

Two Private Sermons from the Reverend Dr. Small, Surprised by Coni, Denise, and Me One Saturday in the Sanctuary of the Southside Community Church of God

I

The minister said, "Hell is for angels . . .
Sin is unhealthy . . . Blues are my colors . . .
Women sewed banners who couldn't afford pictures . . ."
And faith—I think he said—is mathematical.
He said anyone's mother is his mama,
he doesn't scare with damnation
those who need joy, said daughters and nieces
leaving home were saved in patchwork pieces.
Said he was the worst of us. In the turquoise-
carpeted sanctuary claimed he'd done
things he'd never tell. Leaves a door open
when he counsels women. Always guards a corpse.
Said so standing beside a sack of Ajax and Chore Boys:
Saturdays he cleans the church of all the evil he absorbs.

II

When tall Reverend Small knelt on the Topeka quilt,
his index-tips strumming remembered shirts
condensed to diamonds, stitch-stacked
into pyramids, he said,
"Yes, yes, that's *it.*" And when he rose
out of his reflection he began a sermon
during which he couldn't keep his eyes from it.
And when we spread
before him the outreach of the twelve-bar quilt
he said, "That's my mama, yes, that's Mama,"
and from his height thought long into it,
its strong square

cycle he had seen his mother move through.
He preached that evolution was like rolling logs
from mountaintops, like expecting—
at bottom—a log cabin;
we laid out Willia Ette Graham's "Infinity
Log Cabin." "Look," I wondered, "how the center's
in the lower left-hand corner." "That's
normal," he pronounced,
"that's right." And he pointed to the blues
between the heavy, fiery reds. "The blues—
not the brights—
they're our colors," he said.

10

Artists

1

Hip calls

> "Take out your false teeth, Mama,
> Let Daddy suck your gums"

a word—

> "It was already a word
> and I just wrote the rest of the song."

Fish skeletons in his van's wastebasket
might be going
to be a word. They are almost teeth,
they have been sucked clean.

I know what a word *was*.
Now it is always

something for him to finish.

Magic Sam told Hip Linkchain
he needed more than other people's songs.

> "So I wrote ten.
> I just record my own now."

"How did those words
come to you?"

"Out of a clear blue sky."

I'd heard him play
in the dark of a lounge.
Indirect lighting?
Direct unlightedness.

"Out of a clear blue sky."

2

William Dawson, sitting in sawdust,
eighty-seven, nearly hidden
by a large Aretha Franklin
that he built,

said he "just carved"
although he'd never carved before.
He awakened
where form is.
He awoke
in the void.

He paints
how he could raise buildings now,
each roof with a balloon
in which it speaks for itself.

Buddhi, noesis, shih, satori,
deadline, grasp, imperative, prajna.

A purple bird,
red-speckled yellow crow.

What you feel,
how you see things.

"Bird on a Porch,"
on a human house smaller than a bird house.

The commanding bird is sudden knowing.
Mr. Dawson stands under it

in his tiny door.
He was born

recollecting it.

3

Because she changes
every myth she coins,
Yvonne Wells is saying to her studio guests,
    "God sits on His thorn,"
and she has positioned His purple halo
above Christ's crown of
bleeding rickrack.
    A thorn is a pinnacle.
    And as she races to tell
her fast-manifesting narratives,
so little seems
invented before her moment.

Her hot iron falls on the rug
and even that accident
of melted yarns
she quilts

and scripts, naming it "Branded."

A third creation is an odalisque
and shows her procreation's core.

This concocting started
one day when her story-told children had grown; she saw

anyone could be possessed
but isn't,
afraid maybe

to welcome every message,
to quilt a cross one day and a come-on the next
according to signals

from an unsquirming
hard-assed
god.

Suspension: Junior Wells on a
Small Stage in a Converted Barn

As the phobic said: it is torture
to leave the land, to feel distance
between bridge-body and bay-water.
And the way she feels in that slow crowded lane

a listener feels hearing the falling-space
from a voice's full clothing to its thin bones
although his harp is cables
wavering and secure.

Early set tied tight. Late set—the audience shifts, baffled
with his fun: a long disassembly
of bars, and then he rides a sideman,
forces music out of others younger,

forces trouble up and out of consolation.
He tears a note, makes rags of others,
uses them to shine the sound waves
at the far end of the bridge.

"We cannot experience that storied head
in which Apollo's eyeballs ripened like . . . "—
like what?—is it honor, accuracy,
not to finish it? Don't sentence? How

the smallest gesture, little
backpedaling dance or yowl,
is distilled from all the crushed. Like cider.
Like apple-scent. Then sweet courtesy:

"May I say something?" Then the howl.
The little yodel that hovers,
black-throated sparrow, easy in its own extremes,
not knowing whether to land

by the person begging its winter ground
with seeds. It is followed
by grinding, a good groan,
and phrasing low but on toes,

like the farm cat snooping in the bass drum hoop.
And then remorse —
a scrapping of takes, though each began
with leap and bite.

It is not fear or distance that incompletes his songs,
vaporizes them mid-melisma:
song is denied its beautiful death, its resolution,
yet I'm left with resolve —

deny endings to any song, I'll hold the threads.
To yourself you are always live,
but an audience terminated
by show-end and song-end

is falsely complete: the voice-search goes on,
you show them, sounding out
beginnings and middles tonight, the fertile middle
of the night. No last dawn-azure word.

You can't stop singing,
pure gist, suspension. Your holdings,
a sung estate of fragments, remain unabridged.
And you'll be incomplete but never still,

abandoning in favor, in favor of, always.
This is how it must be to make a language,
hands filling out phrases,
silences

each one different from the next. . . .

But of course he was accused,

of sampling. Of tasting a song and putting it back.

And these fragments flew him over the plank walk   over the mud
to his dressing room   the way birds (sparrows after the thaw
—a pair of Old World house sparrows
yesterday in a city gas station   on an aberrant
rescindably warm February noon   almost all the snow
melted except that plowed into piles and iced)   the way birds
pick up from a gutter a straw   a piece of cigarette pack
cellophane   a blade of grass and fly it to   their unfinished nest

Blues in the Joy of the
Fourth of July, Dusk, Crissy Field,
San Francisco

We are the host of people who don't sing
but breathe in, suspiring cheap cupped spirits,
cheer upward from the muddy front row,
the sung-to under the chord of white, red, and blue.

Star on his turban, star over his head,
the thinned man singing where the stage drops away
outsings impatiently growling cannons
poised to the north by the awe of the bay.

Hundreds of boats light up in strings
of incandescence floating, tying up the air.
While draped in bundles of phosphorescent whips,
vendors want to sell

the thing that makes them beautiful.
And between songs the smell of launched light
and its popping sound, proteiform smoke
in faces of wind, a new lavender bomb of sparks,

of details, everyone sighing a roar. Ages
of voices run together. But it is
the singer's one voice, ropy, pulling, saying:
A voice must be old, a voice compounded daily,

split, doubled, rolling with cobbles
like a mine under the sea, its sweetness kept

as a matrix for roughness; a voice shivering,
declarative, sent on ahead. Alleging. It must be

first-person, closing in. Then his simplified
speaking voice saying,
"As soon as we're through here
I'm playing at Eli's."

Then strangers' voices as the night gets older —
"We have to stick together.
It looks like My Lai."
Why that? Why die tonight in other history?

The signature changes —
and he's gone backstage, leaving
miles of crowd kind because happy,
polite when sparks, slide-chords, and sax

are over and we drag the holiday up the hill,
rustle the littery map of the city,
arrive home under the motel's neon light-script
where later I look down to see a bird-wide purple-pink

hibiscus tropical by the ice machine.
More than thumb-to-finger across, blooming
as if to catch leaners from the balconies.
And out of it I am still hearing

Sonny Rhodes naming himself in blue,
voice designating itself, putting its own name

in its song. And the voice—
the years' erosion and increase,

adult life,
singing what really happened to him, the old—
older—pain and pain that gets old
in his house without love,

shivering even "the plants around the room. . . . "
A name he's changed to be more musical, a voice
of perfect ruin, ministering, gambling
on drinking, loneliness, lovelessness, and union.

Dancer to J. J. Malone and The Texas Twisters, Caspar, California

His face is the only dish left of its set.

A single flower is floating
above the crack in it.

Half the night he is the sole dancer on the floor.

Going home, the road a brush stroke along the cliffs,
I see one seal swimming in full moonlight.

I remember a woman in green interrupting,
reaching to take the man as partner.

He kept perfect time,
light on his feet, light of hand while clapping.

One woman in black tights groveled
a dance beneath the star.

You could see a long way clear
down the coast in that round moon-eye.

I had sat still and did not dance
but did not feel that I wasn't dancing —

because of this man's face,
undimmed,

his plain reflecting face
the blues shone on

and out of in even waves, a whole sea's
drift-bones, dashed plates,

left on the shore
by the last note.

Harmonies for the Alienation of My Daughter

I wish I could put her in the birdhouse.
Evicted from her rented room,
she pushes a wheelchair through rain
when only prowl cars can watch her.
I am tossing, it is no dream
she pushes her belongings through night rain
to someplace wet and cold she will belong.
How have I let this happen?
I wish I could put her in the birdhouse.

Some days she bikes to work,
washes the unmovable man in bed,
cleans the quadriplegic quarterback's
cave and then his parrot's cage,
fastens baby's breath in the paralyzed
woman's hair for the opera.
Some days she comes home fired, lies
down in earphones on the floor,
and cannot cry.

If she is moth-crazy (nice Navaho for mad),
she makes reparations to the moths
by opening the night door to her light.
Then she goes up on the roof,
says it is covered with little white rocks
and mushrooms. Says: "It is so silent."
Says: "The stars are writing a bit
like you but not keeping a file on me
like you." Says: "Mother—

Mother's crazy too."

The Ability to Make a Face like a Spider
While Singing Blues: Junior Wells

Who knows if they sing in their webs
or while hunting—they may never have tried
their voices, and what is a spider throat?
But until we know that, a singer thinking
about a *mean black spider* becomes one
without thinking and intends to race
the winged ones through the stickiest place.
Cock your head; when you squint, the
light will throw you reasonable prey,
what you deserve, a gleam, a solo look,
a song to repair the break of day.

Easter 1979

I remember the crucifixion
that April, the neighbors frozen around it,
those with—on their bumpers—"I Found It."
There would be no resurrection

of the limp brown monkey
my daughter nailed through stuffed wrists
so that its neck muscles languished,
the passioned head fell forward, a lanky

rhesus, evolutionary Jesus.
It draped beside my sign to keep the garbage men
from trampling Gethsemane,
our heartland vegetable garden.

Never less simian in their hats and gloves,
homing churchgoers couldn't tell
blasphemous evil from the mentally ill,
and passing up a scarecrow puffed with bur-oak leaves

reviled the mind that looped a tail
around a hickory-twig cross's central spar,
indicted my girl
so poised so young in arts of sacrifice.

Christ, your abstinence
denied us neighbors more divine,
dilute descendants of the Truth and Life.
We too could have been in your bloodline.

But as it is, when boat-tailed grackles
pray in their unoiled call
on both sides of your effigy,
my only beloved daughter feels

not fright but artistry, not thieves but wings.
And she stands to the side and cackles.

Holy Woman: Pecolia Warner

She said she looked at moving objects
and made a pattern up about them.
In wind, birdhouses nailed to a tree,
mailboxes to a roadside grove of posts.
Saw a ripple descend to trouble
deeper water. Watched a tape reel spin
a vision around. Then, *at home*,
she squirmed the pieces into place
(her autograph brushstroke), built a thousand
quilts with her consortium of hymns
and needles. All this thread streaming
in the face of those who scorn our contemplation,
all this quickening the current of a star
by striking argyle space on argyle fire.

Illusion from a Quilt by
Louise Williams

Three Paris models from the back,
leaning together, and life begins
well into adulthood when the soul
enters the imitation of the body
collected of black circles and anemone stems.
Posture: haute shambles.
And yes, they're stuffed
with long underwear.

"There was something aesthetically
pleasing about it."
Yet the hand hurt and the makings slid.
It was just energy,
in building blocks and billows,
as if she were forced
to feel and spread open
cloth-covered autobiographies,
to flatten Grandmother and combine her,
to touch but rip
the hem out of her garment. . . .

Appliqué Tulip Quilt from Kansas

*"This bright cheerful spring quilt was
made in the Thirties by a black
woman."*
                                        —label pinned to quilt

*"The present is like the first time
we remember."*
                                        —Francis Ponge

Even great movements of the clouds
   acknowledge that spot
      by the back door,
   a little garden plot
with drawing power.
                              There, spring falls
upward from the mint-green
   depths of the Depression—
      tulips, thirty-one,
   red, fawn-nectarine,

   rimmed by a guardrail
      as pink as medicine
in spoons. The tulips slide,
   slip, big gown heads
      strain to balance,
however deft at showing off.
   Their leaves rush,
      rock the silence,
   cat stalking a dove
(fur rubbing, wing-escape

      creaking).
Then a top strip throws

the planted rows
all off, misaligning, unregimenting.
  She had a need to excite
    tulips' need to paw.
  As conservator, I crawl,
hand-lens, tweezers, yellow
border urging all the while:
  "Gather her filaments

    too from the dark
side of our quilt, the day-
lily, squash-blossom side
    (that dark a gleam)."
And I do: her silver-blue
  and black hairs, eras,
    equally in it,
  having curled up into
  this flowering cure
    for winter

    and held,
  loosely, supplely,
like a hand-stitched seam.
They will be held in reserve,
    unrusted
  cultivator tools,
while strange heirs, whoever cares,
  crawl on, sleep under,
bulbs doubling in this underground.
  Though waking is inevitable,

is it into her absence
or her present? Century's end—
still in this earth of Holland,
    Turkey, Dahomey, Kansas,
        the longing is born
to be appledoorn, red emperor,
    to grow as she conceived
    her park, her curtilage,
        to flourish:
            weedless.

Designating Duet

I. Putting Your Name in Your Blues

A voice—braided, truth-spilling, close in,
a voice mentioning itself, putting its own name
in its songs

When you voice a song with your own name in it,
and you must add that name, someone else
wrote the song

When you write the song with your name in it,
you give yourself that name,
you change your name
into a song of a name

So that if no announcer designates you,
a listener will know who is shaping
the throat of the song

So that you sing to an old song
new intimacy,
hand over your name to a blues
your name makes as new as it is old

So that the vibrations of your sung name
are distinguished from anyone's
stone-cold name in the rain,
even one that is climbed by wild rose

So that nothing corrodes
your name in time

because your name is sung
as time itself

So that you will never have to wonder
who will sing you,
Sonny Rhodes, Young Bob, O.B.,
The Kid, Milton, Eddie C.

II. Names Not on Quilts

Unwritten work,
used like good words. Unsigned
but orange, blue, pink,
if those are signs.

Lovenice Seals
Motell Jackson

Just one — J. B. Jeters —
and clearly in red
on a buckling sampler.
(This naming is called
friendship.)

Oweatheria Jones
Omega Taylor

On others just as riotous
no designation.

Ebony Jones
Ivory Jones

Would it be like
scratching your name
in your own garden? —
notarizing leaves?

                Queen Esther Brown
                Everleola Smith

Plunge in the sewing needle,
finer than a pen:
openings fill
with the ply of your name.

                Arkeledelpha Washington
                Starling Jackson

Insect letters,
ephemerid's immortality,
winged alphabet as heirloom.

                Floy Zeal Johnson
                Victory White

Your mother didn't
name you Fame.
But your name, a scrap.
Your name, bright orange.

                Birdaree Williams
                Wonderose Lewis

Mysterious-Shape Quilt Top, Anonymous, Oklahoma

Then a shape appeared to her,
which she could not slight,
so that she repeated it, each time
petitioning different colors
to carry it, the light load
of this bubble with points and turrets,
prismatic with surface tension.

It is summer in the heart of the country.
No birds
resemble this twirled shape. If a fish,
it would have to be a fish without a tail
or any eye. Yet its outline is like
a cat's eye, tipped up like that.
The cat's eye floats in a square
she stitches onto yesterday's news,
THE MARLOW REVIEW, THURS * * * 1944.

A canoe-
shape floating and turning in the heat.
She doesn't even have thread; she has
a needle big enough for string.
Has string, white, red.
The forms are spindle-shaped, bright-banded, full.
Short-pointed boat shuttles, bay leaves.
She wants to make the shape
ninety-six times, in the heat, on her lap.

What is it to her?—banded like ellipses
she'll never see: shark coprolite,
Lunar Dove Snail. Yet, she *will* see them—

she will make them. Shapes for whirling,
figures that spin or dive. And on
the back of one —

    DRESS SHOES, patents, turf tans. . . . $2.98
      Now is the time to
      select a gift for the
      boy in Service

and holding together another —

      hope that the worms
    will leave you the lower half of the
    ear at least

and behind one boat —

    Rock Island Gasoline

      car disappointments

and behind one eye —

    CABLE FROM GEORGE DOUGLAS
    IDLETT TELLS HE IS WELL
    IN JAPANESE MILITARY PRISON

and behind another eye —

The Victory
        six jars
        of pickl

and behind one eye-spindle —

                preaching the
                and power. He
                every night,
                positions. He
                and sing

and behind one sea-snail shape —

                Mrs. Walter Pounds served refreshments

and behind one laurel leaf —

                the underground to Lond
                the Nazi begins to suspect
                true love, the Commando, is
                her little Norwegian village

and behind another leaf-eye soul-shape —

                the amazing

—dispatches from the world she didn't create.

But the world she fashioned —
blouse-print sewn against skirt-print

like women in a crowded place, a depot,
a wedge of wives heading for the gate.
Or mothers and babies bumped from planes,
a war's priorities.

Like what remains of Sappho, the *Marlow Review*
jumps word to syllable, seeming to speak full.
And the reconstructed cloth of the mysterious
piecer
stretches on the reverse, tells all it can
on the wordless, every-color-
in-the-book topside.

You Ask for My Book of Poems,
Which You Cannot Read

You prop yourself up with that book you asked for
and see that it starts with an *S*,
the next letter is *T*, and so on.
Maybe the shadows of leaves come in the room
and you wonder why there is no alphabet
of *their* shapes, several species
needed to spell a meaning.
                              You
hold the book and I hope you like it.
I am afraid you will not like it,
that even when the snow comes,
looks up through the window it passed going down,
you'll mull over your bruised ideal
of how the book should sound.
                              Nevertheless
you have reading friends read it again to you,
which makes typeface seem like words,
words seem as if they're from
a heart you know.
                              And now as you hold the book,
the name of its author rubs along your lifeline,
the small serious face of its author
nests in your palm.

We Were Waking

We were waking on the floor of a little cabin.
So that each waking would be happy
we had pinned a white field of yellow stars
over the false-bamboo shades, their broken strings
and empty pulleys.
Dazzling primary stars.
Nonetheless, you were soon thinking
of prison yards and friends' ghosts,
and my eyes were filling
over a friend who'd lost the will to eat—
a fiftyish six-foot man
with a gun in his van.
He'd become ethereal and
we were waking too fast.

That day we would spot the ghostly
snowy plovers
moving close around each other
on an abandoned tract of beach.
Why was it vacant? Because farther on
a magnet fixed the people,
young and standing,
and closer one could see especially
the boy with the purple hair.
Plum or color of plum*flesh*, quite a beautiful
oil-on-water shade. And
at his feet, another boy in a black and green
wetsuit, lying flat.

A woman was bringing her force
to his lungs and his heart.

Quietly one plover watched the other,
serene in the rough sand.

But for now, we leaned half-upright
in bed
thinking of those other things
from the recent past,
things that later would have to be weighed
against drowning and
courtship of plovers.

I weigh them now.
They accept gravity,
all of them. And heavy, heavy
as I am
I show no weight.

Millionaire Records

He knew certain numbers that are not in a book:
If you have five doo-wop singers
    and one of them dies on the road,
can they still go on?

How many did you say there were? Yes, they can do it.
Now, if there were four
    and just three now . . .
Story problems. Many like that.

And he gets them all right: *Winter takes*
a lot of them, or *That's the way*
    Richey wanted to go, playing
the last set for his last set.

His own irradiation came in song-form; it took
four or eight minutes —never five or ten.
    He wrote not one
but two "Millionaire Blues."

So the label would be Millionaire Records,
on which we would expect to hear
    more of the math he picked
for Blues King—suddenly a measure

with five beats and, just when the band
prepared for that again, a bar
    with two and a half.
It threw the whole session off—

rock bass player never got it right—
and so our artist grabbed a spectator
    waiting to record his own—
He'll have it in him (on one

basis only, the stranger's equal color)—
who patched the track at once.
    And later, with a minister's
tone of consecration, *I'll make money*

for you, he told Millionaire's backer,
so sure of his worth when wobbly-hipped
    and hoarse he still
planned to make the album lying down.

He'd play for free, sidemen with no bank accounts
for one hundred fifty cash up front.
    Then talk changed to the price
of an electric razor for a weakening hand,

unshy on the cost of an enema. *One hundred*
ninety-nine, one hundred fifty-one,
    one hundred seven:
his newest weight loss seemed a prime

to identify with, not mass but essence
hallowed in the universe. He'd speak
    each diminution with
astonishment. But he ached on hearing

his three years' airplay royalty: four dollars
eighty-five cents. His mother's church
        took up a collection:
forty-two in change—he is pleased.

Those millionaires, he says, *like Cosby and Oprah,*
doesn't any of it get down to us.
        So he needs a loan,
he tells his drummer over the phone.

It keeps sounding like *I need a lung.*
Back in June, inside a juke
        with Christmas decorations up,
not in anticipation but in perpetuation,

swagged all around, he played six hours
for a mere thirty-five and the force
        to thrum linoleum floors.
He ate bean soup, dumplings, anything

you boil, for sixty a month.
Summoned, *Write this down. I'll cut*
        "Mary Lou," "Dirty, Dirty,"
"Give Me Your Dresser (I Want to Get into

Your Drawers)," "Long-leg Turkey" —
originals—before diagnosed. So someone
        he danced with once
on the road called, Get the words, Nick and Mari,

get the words, Sister Tish, won't the nurse
get the words no one's ever heard,
    that were to break
Millionaire Records just even? But neither

his reverend, nor three of his wives,
nor Tail Dragger, Kansas City, Huckleberry Hound,
    each of whom laughed
as he willed at his bedside, begged from him

in time the words to all his lost numbers.
—Yet because, once, he hollered
    into a tape recorder
in a French hotel, to play with time,

here, in his pantherous voice, among
his effects, turns up one
    of the lost originals.
He's working out the melody,

having thought up the verse first,
minor key acoustic struck hard—
    I'm like a long-leg turkey
running from a wide-foot goose—.

Luckily he never tried to say that
on his deathbed. Here is how he shaped
    inspiration, tape by tape
and roost by roost,

on tour. *You don't know where you are
but you go home*, he soothed.
    And here he's going home,
who sang not notes

but wide cries, floodings, fishtailings,
and swipes. The found song sounds like that,
    his home voice, field voice,
echoing off the mansions.

Bad Mother Blues

When you were arrested, child, and I had to take your pocketknife
When you were booked and I had to confiscate your pocketknife
It had blood on it from where you'd tried to take your life

It was the night before Thanksgiving, all the family coming over
The night before Thanksgiving, all the family coming over
We had to hide your porno magazine and put your handcuffs undercover

Each naked man looked at you, said, Baby who do you think you are
Each man looked straight down on you, like a waiting astronomer's star
Solely, disgustedly, each wagged his luster

I've decided to throw horror down the well and wish on it
Decided I'll throw horror down the well and wish on it
And up from the water will shine my sweet girl in her baby bonnet

A thief will blind you with his flashlight
                              but a daughter be your bouquet
A thief will blind you with his flashlight
                              but a daughter be your bouquet
When the thief's your daughter you turn your eyes the other way

I'm going into the sunflower field where all of them are facing me
I'm going into the sunflower field so all of them are facing me
Going to go behind the sunflowers, feel all the sun that I can't see

One Way She Spoke to Me

I would say, "Whisper." And she could
never figure how to do it. I would say,
"Speak louder," into the phone, nor
could she raise her voice.

But then I found such a whisper, the trail
as she began to write to me in snails,
in silver memos on the front door,
in witnesses to her sense of touch.

Home late, I found them slurred
and searching, erasing the welcome
she'd arranged them in:
H—twelve snails. I—seven or six.

They were misspelling it,
digressing in wayward caravans and pileups,
mobile and rolling but with little perspective,
their eyestalks smooth as nylons on tiny legs.

I raised her in isolation. But it is these snails
who keep climbing the walls. For them, maybe
every vertical makes an unending tree—
and every ascension's lovely.

Why else don't they wend homeward to ground?
But what do *we* do? We are only a part
of a letter in a word. And we are on our
bellies with speech, wondering, wondering slowly,

how to move toward one another.

Suit and Tie

Sewing up shadows:
she has no inkling what it's like to be this man.
Is it wrong, too dainty, not to want to imagine?
She keeps doilies on the bedstands;
men's suits, quilted, on the bed.
Her Italian beads wait to dress her,
cold rain in a pool circling to rise.
And, in a basket, his tossed ties
spiral: seventy she'll overlap,
slap down, lavish into a quilt.
Both these covers heavy, like columns fallen.

Some afternoons she abstracts herself:
she shadows glimmers through the suit quilt.
It is like entering a forest,
prickling with her first bee-sting,
setting up house in a hollow stump.
She takes her grandmother's
one-cup measure to water moss.
Another day, it's like entering a forest—older,
when she is pregnant and she tastes
her fear of the mother bear's
rival like-mindedness.

Some days she lays out bowties, ascots,
ties of discredited widths,
arranges their slinky, protracted lips
(as long as arms) to meet.
A colossus neither female nor male,
a power she finds unlike any
clothed (so well she knows the clothes).

51

She studies the two spectrums—
wool lichen-glum slacks, black gabardine
she mended once, machine-sewing
like a tractor; and those flippant ties
that swim and ripple over, through, each other,
confluences of red-brown, blue-brown glazing clays.
Half the world that is not me, she thinks,
knows these but can't lie down in them;
I'll make a man's work incubate our sleep;
I'll make it cleave to the nest.

And so it is, one room in her house.
She can always find another bed
with summer blouses trimmed to facets, lenses, planes—
to True Lovers' Knot, to Variable Star—
those gussets, darts, pleats, and gores
of garden prints. There is always that sunshine
before she chooses to sleep in the woods.

Or it is this—

      "I am seventy-three years old. I can't
   ramble the woods to find flowers like I used to.
     My children all tell me don't leave the yard.
  I am almost in woods, can't see a light anywhere
       at night. I wish you could see this part
 of the world, would love to ramble for wild flowers
with you. I have permission from the paper company
   that owns the land to gather any flowers I want,
       if I had someone to keep me
         from getting lost
          in the woods."

Three Purses of a Nomadic Woman

for Jean Valentine

I will pass the purses over the border,
the pouches of duiker and rabbit skins,
empty one inside the other.

The stranger will empty money into my hands.

I will purchase a farmer's wife's
used plastic bag with a clasp.
Then I will smell the free animals better

as they pass closely at night —

           ❧

                    as here the sparrows
cross the ashen sky,
rush, reflutter, fan to
perches small enough for them,
and I wonder why
is this finch-quick woman
selling her symbols?
And why are those symbols wheels
or starfish she's never seen in her desert,
sewn in slow-water green
and redwing-epaulet brights
to hides? Why selling her
ostrich eggshell beads
joined into a fringe

or worn across her hair like
white crown-lines on a bush sparrow . . .

&

Is it only we
who hang our white hair
over our dolls,
their blue faces,
their soft heads?

Or, as well, with three scrub brushes
arranged like dolls,
the man who uses them
to brighten up a pall?

&

In one of the purses is a little fragrant pipe,
a segment, apparently, of a pipe,
fragrant as if the old smoke
were putting out a flower,
its first.
It makes me bring my whole body
up to this little pipe
whose draw would be narrow
for an ant.
I wait there, at the access
as if the essential vein
from her lung to her heart
might suddenly flow through it.

We have lifted clutches of mussel shells into heaps
miles inland. Theirs seems
an opalescent way to grow.
I'm wondering if X
thinks he grows in opalescence, if Y
sees by it
under floods.
These are humans I am thinking of . . .

*

Denise runs her fingers over the dry
swimming-pool cells of the blue-green starfish
she pulled from a wrapped box.
Her five fingers on its five rays.
There is concentration too
in the reshaping of ostrich eggs
to disks this tiny.
A woman works at the lathe
and her grandchild pushes a coal
into her hut's grass walls, kindles all her riches.
The ostrich must be asked again
for her endowment.

*

I have the face
you are used to.
I go to the border.

I know someone
will look to my hands
and accept
the three faces
beautiful in my hands.

≈

In the morning, showing the powderpuff sling to Denise, I find a
second puff. Old veld herbs pour out. That evening, Susan discovers one
cushion has a tail and is approximately mouse-size. Some mammal, a
powderpuff with a tail! "A long-nosed mouse . . . informs life of things
not seen . . . one of the earliest of our . . . images of intuition."

≈

Perhaps the skin
is not sealed,
need not be
if it is. The sheath
of this being
held up to the light
shows windows,
breakages,
star-points. I am
looking from inside
the purse. There is
a horizon
in its depth. She
was aware of
all its perforations
could bear.

&sa;

Touching the holes
in this skin pocket.
Their stamina,
their web—
my hand is caught.

&sa;

Do you want to know what I've kept for myself?
Take these three
and keep always
that longing to know.

&sa;

The grub-stick made
as subtle as possible, embellished
with ant-thin tracks, rills
of ants trickling
toward the point

which will harrow the hidden, quiet, root-attached life
and its poison—

&sa;

I go to the border again.
I can pass over it any way I wish.
I do not want to sell anything.

&a.

I listen to the way substance is questioned. The content of a woman's story, a wife watching her husband lie while buying a piano. Or one bird's durable frail form accepting a pedestal that will break in the next windstorm. A powderpuff a mother's son killed with a little noose. A ninety-one-year-old sleeping in her front yard because someone tried to kill her in her home.

&a.

Sometimes I buy cloth
just to see
not what it might be made into
but what the unmade is made of.

&a.

I come up to a man on the border.
I can, like a spirit transpiercing walls,
with impunity move back and forth
across a space that has to no one else
a single opening. Only
my bloodline is not asked
to imagine a confine, a barricade.
I approach a man who cannot take
another step forward.

❧

Unlike any flying creature, unlike any running animal, unlike
grass seed,

unlike me,

the person I greet must edge toward this limit
under scrutiny,
with denial, caution, justification,
for search,
and must halt at this line, reach into
no other realm.

❧

Dawn has what I want.
The graces of flimsiness.
My children play
with grass horses.

❧

I watch the man walk away on his one side of the border.
He has several animals in his hands.
The purses are all we did not eat of them.
I sewed them back into shapes of torsos and hearts
so they could go on containing, embracing,
holding, surrounding.

If there is some beauty left,
only the hand lighter than power
can touch it,
tensility of spirit,
finer than the boundary it splits.
Stretching through all,
its mouse nerve insists
I live by
its insistence.

Women and Objects

As the bereft, the biochemically
   woebegone, the work-hollowed
       lose
     the sticky surface *things*
     adhere to, these souls'
   possessions roll to the walls
     and breathe among themselves
      of how empty-
handed their owner seems. And she stops
     collecting, balks at this
    livelihood of acquisitions,
    the embellishing gestures

    of the sport: the extravagant
      scrawl on checks, clutched mail,
reconstellating, collocating
    by distinguishing marks. All that
       vaporizes
as if it never meant whatever
   color means or harvest bounty
or vivacity of form on form
     on soul.
   She is a woman without
objects now and her finger neither dials
     nor points.

    The herring gulls wheel
   over black water. Muslin-
   yellow sand empillows the hips

of the winter visitor at early sundown.
     Nerves
  of one fingerprint know
  the nacre of a shell;
  while the thumb supports
  ridged outer roughness
planted with a small sea weed:
     "And thus
I have already violated the absentee

     in me
  with a first object," she
reflects over a postcard that night at home
  (a close-up of shells—
  Greetings from the Coast).
  By then she's borrowed quite a few
  of the sea's belongings. Drying,
   the objects consign
sea crystals to her mat, her tabletop,
    her bed.
The chafing begins to hallow her.
  "Women and Objects,"

    my Day of the Dead
     figure types
(her hair is starlit blue; her cheekbones
   the basic cheer behind
  the absent smileable musculature).
    "Always,"
  she remembers,
  "the disorder of paper stacks

and copied birds (spun, potted, painted, carved),
    of favorite baskets, Anne's
painting of woven straps of fishtraps —
      elected

objectification of someone else's
      favored object.
   At the time one is alive
the clutter becomes intolerable, you blame
    yourself for aggregating
    visions that build no tower,
    that architect a rubble
    (fascinating in detail)
of mineral tones and scrumbly surfaces
    with no museum-clear
    results. You and your objects!
      —the fish-ripe

    sea sponges that puff
    in garden alcoves when it rains,
    the mushroom ten years old that walks
across a path-stone in heavy dew.
     It's all permissible
      from death,"
    she's typing on her Underwood
    that is a jumble
of mussel shells clinging to her desk
     which is the sea . . .
"Credit your chaos with categorization
if you can organize by beauty

equally as by use
(because each object shares
both fairnesses the same).
   Slovenliness
is golden and mean
in which you still recall
the broken fingers of the doll,
   torn drills in writing
with a very fine hand, and the hard fling away
   of *Do not touch*.
You wanted to keep something,
   make something, buy;

if not icons to worship,
   images
of an imagination that has worshiped.
   Only hatred of art
   demands that idols be destroyed,"
she taps upon the driftwood-
   coal fire
of her Underwood as its light dies
   and she keeps warm
   just thinking
what the bones of her hands
   will report . . .

Women and Vision

One hundredth of what we see:
the near-blind daughter of the decorator,
row 6 seat C, beside me on the flight
to Providence.

A hundred times what we see:
Faye's schizophrenic teenager hallucinating.
Faye's own cross-hatched, net-stocking drawings;
the decorator's pique-assiette.

Kay can't see the route numbers on city buses
except in quadruplicate. She uses a camera—
steady, at home. She poses leathery, wrenched,
dried tomatoes,

clarinet keys for seeds,
and flashes the arrangement no one places
in black and white.
Ava and her hat—envisioning her hat

looks better on Randell, urging Randell
to paint his portrait in her hat
(one scarlet feather
scythes down the back).

Mary's Alabama patch quilt—big, pale, and vague:
I've stared into it for months. Like hitching
with a trucker through coastal fog, grayed chaparral,
to a year of my life.

Mary's windbreaker factory-remnant cruciform
design with swatches of washcloth.
Weight on her sleep, rooster and chimes.
Then always hoisted away by morning.

Not interested
in decisions made *before* construction;
I want only to know
about those who decide

with their last few scraps—when,
in a sense, it's *too late.*
Penny is helping men
force their new transsexual voice

into breathiness. "Just like
Jean Valentine's," she says. "Perfect!"
Kerry forces his womanly vision
into a sheath-dress, clematis clinger affectionate

to his new incarnation. Black Moon
is plumbing her *Bloodshower,*
a proto–Red Riding Hood theme—
going back in the myth

to when she had to rescue herself.
Eight pints of her own will run through it
until splashing has enameled the tile.
Black Moon is wan, the origin.

But this is not forced vision. Forced vision
is Eva refusing her blood pressure drug
so she intoxicates on her own body.
Forced vision

is Margaret pixilating into ladies and harridans,
each using a different hue of pen
in their one diary, her own identifying weapon
(baby talk; a swipe of glass), and separate antonym

to "Margaret." But at least they forced it:
one hundredth of what's to see
invites the aspectless, some abject ones,
to cover their gaze.

The dollmaker enlarged the eyes
of the vodun figure for foresight: green
as dangling wisteria pods in viny shade,
as the empty theater in a pepper.

They are telescopes of clay, glazed orbs.
The doll's shell breasts—
moonsnail, urchin—are two different
temperatures. Touching my skin its moss

hair feels feline (like the calico, Hailey,
licking gingham in Mary's quilt). Its mystic two-stick
body has a stake in inspiring change
in a life too static, chaste,

unready to flick the highlights of its evolution
past assurances it could come back.
Black Moon goes on to paint
porterhouses, T-bones, sardonyx

with gristle, around the room a wainscot
of cleavers and mincing knives.
"We've got to get beyond this," cries Elizabeth;
but we won't give more blood, we haven't

even given ours. Nellie Mae has painted
her last faintly outlined fish: from now on
hers are beet-celled, jet-gilled, checkerboard-scaled
in waters where they will exist,

she glosses, in the future. Inez
outlines lake-size frontal eyes
on profiles, lashes for rushes,
testifies from prison that she draws

to guard herself from *bad girls*,
her line a brook purling to that world
where she was murderous.
Or where Black Moon's faucet turns, her maroon

standing in for clear water.

Willia Ette Graham's Infinity Log Cabin Quilt, Oakland, 1987

"... all symmetries are based on the assumption that it is
impossible to observe certain basic quantities, which we shall
call 'nonobservables.' Conversely, whenever a nonobservable
becomes an observable, we have a symmetry violation."
—T. D. Lee, physicist

"That's normal."
—Reverend Robert Small

Probably
she set out
to make a rainbow
one can't

get out
from under,
its edges
layered on raw,

bulges overlapped
to nap
down smooth.
Here and there

she stored
spare
triangles,
beside a flower path

or in
an abandoned yellow ray.
Ripples
in her universe

have angles,
and the center
is a long
way down.

A ring
around a quilt
is a square.
And the questionable

bands
the inspirational—
there is always
something

farther out,
its own zone
and home.
Blue heavens

resolve
into cheap
chartreuse.
An earth-

patch starts
a day, seams it
to night.
But suddenly

her stripes
reverse
the field,
breach

the mirror.
She finds
the remnant shop
of nonobservables.

The most terrible
lane of cloth
she faces —
it is travesty

to posit any
finer fabric
in its place.
And so

the aureate
and anti-aureate
sashes pulse
from the

cornered center
as if
from the splash
of a log cabin.

Infinity
does not
exaggerate:
it is a large object

readable
across a lake,
then foldable, carryable
under an arm.

When one
opens it
again, everything
pending appears.

Some Metaphysics of
Junior Wells

18 September 1987

1

A night universe scallop-edged with his faces—
surprise mostly—one shock unmasking another,
one, out of still water, splashing another.

Astonishment, as if a bird had landed on his head.

Amazement stronger than awe, more aggressive than awe.

A day universe? "Promoters pissing on your head,
trying to make you believe it's raining."

2

He says he's been "fucking up the whole tour"—everyone's
mad at him; but tonight he is thrilled to feel
as well as he does.

The dusk, his partner thinks, is Southern:
"The mosquitos bring the air."
Full moon, farmland, horse, and goat.
Junior is as light

as three nighthawks.
                    Singing with his arms,
he migrates, assuming the wind-brushed form
for aerial carriage.

3

He washes his hands
around his harp;
fist hits his heart,
shoots out one long finger.
He looks into one hand,
counts with it, waves,
trills it, it curves like grass,
it signals *Stop*.
One hand is quick on hip,
waggles, clicks; thumbs up,
hand shakes off time,
thumb rolls in and out of fist.
One hand folds in over harp.
A cormorant's wing. Index
makes a #1. He boxes.
One hand flashes, plays
his waist; he shaves
with a hand's edge.
Claps heels of palms, a fist
is something to release; fingertips
kiss his mouth; hand
makes a sign like water.

4

You can make a sound bigger than yourself.
You can sign a sound bigger than yourself.
You can whirl sound around in your mouth.

You can make a music which is only your face in silence.

You can squint your lips and *clock* your tongue.
You can hoot and melodize.
You can never waste a thing.

In right creation there is no waste.
(But the hours before, the living between?)
None. You can add matter to the universe.

In the wind the bird saw several faces.
They were all different, easy to tell apart.
They were Beginning, Birth, Newness, and Dawn.

Ode for the God of Indeterminacy

I

A pheasant at this airport, egrets at that one's rice-edge—
these avatars can be exalting there.
But the night before a flight,
I imagine nothing unharrowing: running through tunnels;

the lightning at the gate; in my grip
paid access to a cancellation.
And I'm always belabored toting the hope
of all our portraits in the plane's portholes—

like chickens crowded in a long barn
in flooded countryside near Carrollton—great barge
of a birdhouse of sacrifices.
I know this god.

II

At a crossroads outside a Yoruba village
a raw mound of earth is not a mortar pile,
not a bank of ant siftings. A chicken
is being sacrificed to it, to mud.

The mud is a shrine—to Eshu, the god
of indeterminacy, odd numbers, asymmetry,
occurrences so singular
you cannot entice them again.

There are odes to deliver here:
the most incomplete is mine.

III

I am riding up I-65 with Louie
Skipper and he asks me
to read psalms. It's been a long time
since my favorite was clear

to me. It is dogwood countryside,
blossoms like paparazzi catch us
as we speed by. I try—
but my tongue crosses memorized King James

with Louie's denomination's new translation
of One Twenty One:
from whence cometh my help
now says *where does my help come from?*

O god as migratory as a swan or a goose,
be mine.

IV

If you spread all your beliefs
crossways to your disbeliefs
the square where they intersect
is holy ground.

Though it is struck from all sides,
it is your hearth, your patch, your junction of amends.

V

I lift up my eyes to the hills
Little aerial roots, where did you hang my death?
I sing a song of ascent
O opener of runways
a tree still drips unseen in the fog,
only the jackrabbit takes off and lands, takes off and lands
The Lord will watch over your coming and going
even as you worship Our Mother of Waters
on the day you are using the tears in your eyes
to hunt for the good things of life
The Lord will watch over your
coming and going
both now
and forevermore

VI

Late evening, backtracking from Birmingham,
drawing up to an intersection in Tuscaloosa,
awaiting a light purple and meaningless to traffic,
we saw a man-size chicken jigging, frantic
in its costume, desperate for
its life or its living, promoting Sav-Mor
with a dance its human
heartbeat couldn't harmonize
with big scratching feet.
No one we could see even moved to aim.
Did it not honor the god's
spirit more to let it live?

VII

At three A.M. just this, words at my hand saying,
*There is a Higher Uncertainty
than the one you feel now,
there is within you
a Higher Powerlessness.*

Its illustration is of bird paths
interlacing, so I can see
they don't go anywhere, it doesn't matter
once they're up in the air.

And I can behold, in the dark, traces
of ways—an unsure word,
a random suffering,
last spring's stumbling lopsided cowbird,
a one-time happy thing—

to serve my god
who doesn't want me wishing,
who fiddles perpetually with my hand,
crossing and uncrossing my fingers.

Landscape with Master Class,
Northern Oregon Coast

From the cabinette's small breather of a deck
I hear the tiny hammering (that can't be
but I look, it *is*, steel-drum-making)
begin the morning across the swale,
the tidal creek, the schoolyard on its brim.
I had thought someone was fastening a downspout.
A seagull, coming in, has similar rhythm
but more of a call, half query, half squall.
I go on pounding sand out of a shoe.

And the students contour plates of tone
into chimes, thinning and widening
timbre openly in the beach-sand softball diamond
where a young writer slept, one summer,
another era, to afford to study
with the writing master. Feldspar over macadam;
beach peas he could have shelled;
blackberries he ate or used to meditate:
he slept there.
                    Now he has lost his master
but others are earning theirs:
seen through a doorway in the gym, this one—
Mr. Mannette—brings his blackberry-green pen
to a steel drum's inner skin, marks an *X*
for the cross of a note, works at the pinch
in an octave, sees his tuner's
wave of perfect reverberation
to know he's hearing it.

They perform for the village in two days.
More frequently, the tide
bulges, drops, unveils—
for the kingfisher on the powerline—
reflecting, outgoing, mountain creekwater.
Later, seawater rides in over it
and the bird must look into it differently,
as one sees through skylights

differently than through portholes.
A red alder leaf falls. It is only August.
Little sawed-off ball-peens tap pitch in.
No nail is driven through anything.

On the bailed-out ebb, beneath the denim,
cloud-agate kingfisher, a student jumps across
to this slack hour's sandbar come to light.
Smooth, saturated, algal and quartz shoal.
She sinks archaeologically with each step,
with her progress toward the marine.
Around her the split creek trails half asleep,
amber cider in a green bottle.
"The octave is moving a little,"

the drum teacher says. By evening,
wearing either a hydrocoral-pink,
whelk-orange yarn beret
or a silver cummerbund folded
like wave sequences counted from a cliff,
each player walks to the concert and bears,
inside, a personal, impure, demiclear note.

Next day we have a chillier, foggier dawn.
Drops are listed on black wires.
The gunmetal gray gym resembles an oil drum
laid on its side, half buried in the sand.
A few graduates stay to tinker but it is over
for a year, the grounds and classrooms bare
with that particular emptiness of savvy
recanting us, never being where we thought
it was, or not existing after all.

But I go closer, anyway, onto the little bridge:
the tide is flowing in so fast
I see a last musician's footprints
under the water.

Two Men Trading Dance Movements at
Tabby's Blues Box and Heritage Hall, Baton Rouge

Whatever is expressive
about clumsiness (bad knees),
   disproportion (potbelly,
putto hands), untaught
   self-portraiture,
wall-hugging, cold
   feet, or stillness—
chilled into models—
   painters must jar
to life,
         we may like this
   more, seeing
how these men start from an uncandescent
   corner by the entry door
(not at the back
   by the restrooms'
mussed, rampageous
   tulip colors)
and match up: two men,
   simply, by image,
but impulse-different, nerve-distinct.

And so, beginning from this vertex,
   the two
open like radiolarians—
   one with blazing glass bones
raving from its nucleus,
   the other living out
of an invisible core

with a burst
of tines (like burrs,
    chinquapin nuts, globefish)
at the globe-surface (wands,
    extrusions, rep of
waffles and honeycombs, cages
    permuting to regalia,
those microscopic bombastic
    laces, cacti, and grilles,
the bizarre—a hairnet over antlers,
    javelins
beside featherstitching), and
    alternate astonishing
each other with outward-firing
    or inward-brawling flurries
of their two repertoires, one
    a medusa disentangling,
the other formal as a Caspian tern.

One morning, later, after
    a downpour, I track raindrops
where hairs on a flume-creased tree-lupine leaf
    roll them into spheres,
and under a hand lens see dancers,
    magnifying partners,
bump the diving-bell edge,
    a tense bay window,
and propel there, a pair
    in a room not yet evaporated.
These two
    are in a tournament

and I recall
    how one man, pearl-three-pieced
and cubist, dances his
    points, lines, angles,
surfaces, and solids,
    then the other,
in work blues, purling,
    water-snaky, suddenly
up through the waist sends a shudder
    into shoulders, forearms, hands over head
to traverse the room
    in a turbidity whipping up something
like the gasp
    at Jules Lion's first New Orleans
daguerreotypes that there is a whole
    re-erected city there
yet every detail — an insect
    on a stone of a cathedral —
can be discerned, lucid in itself.

What esteem
    they are paying each other,
stretching a flat hand out
    to the other's palm, back
and forth all evening until the elegant
    man decides the serpentine
has won, concedes but is so pleased
    he holds the other's grip a moment.
These are not dances
    the world knows; they are inside
explosions, privity,

idiosyncrasy with
molecularly fine technique.
   When paint peels
off Tabby's walls, when the photographs
   of road-brumous singers
curl around their tacks,
   that is how they move,
this is contractual art,
   fleshed fireworks, a making
for the other
   of a signal pointing
away from isolation,
   a countersign that will only work if
aurified by *horror vacui*
   and tavern lamp
and encountered
   round a corner,
a prospect contracting them to be —
   with acutest scope —
infinitesimally
   visible together,
down to
   the winner's work keys
still ringed
   to his belt loop.

Notes

"For St. James, Who Said He Was on Tour with The Emotions": Percy Mayfield's comments are taken from an interview in *Living Blues*, no. 50, Spring 1981. Line 36 is a comment by Walter Pavlich. St. James Bryant was killed in a car accident on December 2, 1988, after a performance in the Midwest. This poem was completed before his death.

"Suspension: Junior Wells on a Small Stage in a Converted Barn": The quoted lines in stanza five are from William Heyen's translation of Rilke's "On an Archaic Torso of Apollo."

"Millionaire Records": The quotations are statements made by Hip Linkchain in private conversation.

"Suit and Tie": The final quote is molded from a correspondent in Elizabeth Lawrence's book *Gardening for Love* (Duke University Press, 1987, p. 152). The actual quilts were made by two women: a turn-of-the-century African-American woman, name unrecorded, from Chicago, constructed the suit quilt; Gerstine Scott of Oakland, California, assembled the necktie quilt.

"Three Purses of a Nomadic Woman": The purses were originally the property of a !Kung San woman; she sold them to an American on the border of Botswana and Namibia.

"Ode for the God of Indeterminacy": Section II uses a narration of Robert Plant Armstrong's in *The Powers of Presence*; section V quotes a few lines from Judith Gleason's translations of African praise poems in *Leaf and Bone*, but other lines in italics are my invention.

"Two Men Trading Dance Movements at Tabby's Blues Box and Heritage Hall, Baton Rouge": Jules Lion, a "free man of color," a portrait painter and lithographer, was the first to exhibit daguerreotype views of New Orleans in that city, March 1840. See *Photography in New Orleans: The Early Years, 1840–1865*, by Margaret Denton Smith and Mary Louise Tucker (Baton Rouge: Louisiana State University Press, 1982).

Acknowledgments

Grateful acknowledgment is made to the following publishers for permission to reprint poems that have appeared previously:

The American Poetry Review: "For St. James, Who Said He Was on Tour with The Emotions"; "Bad Mother Blues"; "Dancer to J. J. Malone and The Texas Twisters . . ."; "Three Purses of a Nomadic Woman"; "We Were Waking"

The American Voice: "Quilt of Rights"

Bakunin: "You Ask for My Book of Poems, Which You Cannot Read"

Field: "Twelve-Bar Quilt"; "Designating Duet"; "Holy Woman: Pecolia Warner"; "One Way She Spoke to Me"; "Two Private Sermons from the Reverend Dr. Small . . ."

Grand Street: "Ode for the God of Indeterminacy"

The Iowa Review: "Artists"

The Kenyon Review: "Suit and Tie"; "Women and Vision"

The Missouri Review: "Easter 1979"

The New Criterion: "Appliqué Tulip Quilt from Kansas"; "Willia Ette Graham's Infinity Log Cabin Quilt . . ."

The New Republic: "The Ability to Make a Face like a Spider . . ."

The Paris Review: "Two Men Trading Dance Movements at Tabby's Blues Box . . ."

The Southern Review: "Illusion from a Quilt by Louise Williams"; "Landscape with Master Class, Northern Oregon Coast"

TriQuarterly: "Suspension: Junior Wells on a Small Stage in a Converted Barn"; "Blues in the Joy of the Fourth of July . . ."; "Mysterious-Shape Quilt Top, Anonymous, Oklahoma"; "Women and Objects"

Woman Poet: The West II: "Harmonies for the Alienation of My Daughter"

The Yale Review: "Some Metaphysics of Junior Wells"; "Quilt Top Discovered at the Muskogee Flea Market . . ."

ZYZZYVA: "Millionaire Records"

Special thanks to Claire Van Vliet of Janus Press for her boxed edition of "Designating Duet"; to the University of California at Davis for research grants for the years 1986–91; and to Eli Leon, Mary Popma, Lynn Rousseau, Marilyn Packer, and Robert Cargo for their expertise with African-American quilts.

Poetry from Illinois

Dear John, Dear Coltrane
Michael S. Harper (1985)

Poems from the Sangamon
John Knoepfle (1985)

Eroding Witness
Nathaniel Mackey (1985)
National Poetry Series

In It
Stephen Berg (1986)

Palladium
Alice Fulton (1986)
National Poetry Series

The Ghosts of Who We Were
Phyllis Thompson (1986)

Moon in a Mason Jar
Robert Wrigley (1986)

Lower-Class Heresy
T. R. Hummer (1987)

Poems: New and Selected
Frederick Morgan (1987)

Cities in Motion
Sylvia Moss (1987)
National Poetry Series

Furnace Harbor: A Rhapsody
of the North Country
Philip D. Church (1988)

The Hand of God and a Few
Bright Flowers
William Olsen (1988)
National Poetry Series

Bad Girl, with Hawk
Nance Van Winckel (1988)

Blue Tango
Michael Van Walleghen (1989)

The Great Bird of Love
Paul Zimmer (1989)
National Poetry Series

Eden
Dennis Schmitz (1989)

Waiting for Poppa at the
Smithtown Diner
Peter Serchuk (1990)

Great Blue
Brendan Galvin (1990)

Stubborn
Roland Flint (1990)
National Poetry Series

What My Father Believed
Robert Wrigley (1991)

Something Grazes Our Hair
S. J. Marks (1991)

The Surface
Laura Mullen (1991)
National Poetry Series

Walking the Blind Dog
G. E. Murray (1992)

The Sawdust War
Jim Barnes (1992)

The Dig
Lynn Emanuel (1992)
National Poetry Series

The God of Indeterminacy
Sandra McPherson (1993)